Francis Frith's

BERKSHIRE
LIVING MEMORIES

photographs of the mid twentieth century

Francis Frith's

BERKSHIRE
LIVING MEMORIES

Nick Channer

First published in the United Kingdom in 2001 by
Frith Book Company Ltd

Paperback Edition 2001
ISBN 1-85937-332-1

British Library Cataloguing in Publication Data

Francis Frith's Berkshire Living Memories
Nick Channer

Frith Book Company Ltd
Frith's Barn, Teffont,
Salisbury, Wiltshire SP3 5QP
Tel: +44 (0) 1722 716 376
Email: info@francisfrith.co.uk
www.francisfrith.co.uk

Printed and bound in Great Britain

Front Cover: Pangbourne, High Street c1955 P5013

AS WITH ANY HISTORICAL DATABASE THE FRITH ARCHIVE IS CONSTANTLY BEING CORRECTED AND IMPROVED
AND THE PUBLISHERS WOULD WELCOME INFORMATION ON OMISSIONS OR INACCURACIES

Contents

Francis Frith: Victorian Pioneer

FRANCIS FRITH, Victorian founder of the world-famous photographic archive, was a complex and multi-talented man. A devout Quaker and a highly successful Victorian businessman, he was both philosophic by nature and pioneering in outlook.

By 1855 Francis Frith had already established a wholesale grocery business in Liverpool, and sold it for the astonishing sum of £200,000, which is the equivalent today of over £15,000,000. Now a multi-millionaire, he was able to indulge his passion for travel. As a child he had pored over travel books written by early explorers, and his fancy and imagination had been stirred by family holidays to the sublime mountain regions of Wales and Scotland. 'What a land of spirit-stirring and enriching scenes and places!' he had written. He was to return to these scenes of grandeur in later years to 'recapture the thousands of vivid and tender memories', but with a different purpose. Now in his thirties, and captivated by the new science of photography, Frith set out on a series of pioneering journeys to the Nile regions that occupied him from 1856 until 1860.

Intrigue and Adventure

He took with him on his travels a specially-designed wicker carriage that acted as both dark-room and sleeping chamber. These far-flung journeys were packed with intrigue and adventure. In his life story, written when he was sixty-three, Frith tells of being held captive by bandits, and of fighting 'an awful midnight battle to the very point of surrender with a deadly pack of hungry, wild dogs'. Sporting flowing Arab costume, Frith arrived at Akaba by camel seventy years before Lawrence, where he encountered 'desert princes and rival sheikhs, blazing with jewel-hilted swords'.

During these extraordinary adventures he was assiduously exploring the desert regions bordering the Nile and patiently recording the antiquities and peoples with his camera. He was the first photographer to venture beyond the sixth cataract. Africa was still the mysterious 'Dark Continent', and Stanley and Livingstone's historic meeting was a decade into the future. The conditions for picture taking confound belief. He laboured for hours in his wicker dark-room in the sweltering heat of the desert, while the volatile chemicals fizzed dangerously in their trays. Often he was forced to work in remote tombs and caves where conditions were cooler. Back in London he exhibited his photographs and was 'rapturously cheered' by members of the Royal Society. His reputation as a photographer was made overnight. An eminent modern historian has likened their impact on the population of the time to that on our own generation of the first photographs taken on the surface of the moon.

Venture of a Life-Time

Characteristically, Frith quickly spotted the opportunity to create a new business as a specialist publisher of photographs. He lived in an era of immense and sometimes violent change. For the poor in the early part of Victoria's reign work was a drudge and the hours long, and people had precious little free time to enjoy themselves. Most had no transport other than a cart or gig at their disposal, and had not travelled far beyond the boundaries of their own town or village. However, by the 1870s, the railways had threaded their way across the country, and Bank Holidays and half-day Saturdays had been made obligatory by Act of Parliament. All of a sudden the ordinary working man and his family were able to enjoy days out and see a little more of the world.

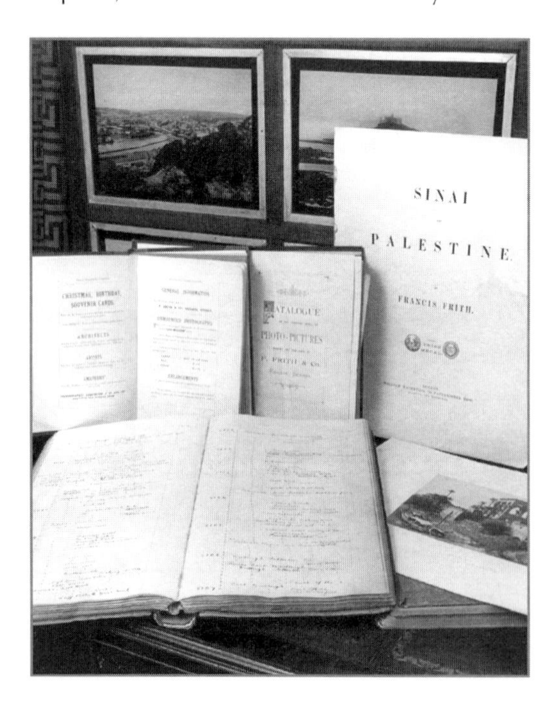

With characteristic business acumen, Francis Frith foresaw that these new tourists would enjoy having souvenirs to commemorate their days out. In 1860 he married Mary Ann Rosling and set out with the intention of photographing every city, town and village in Britain. For the next thirty years he travelled the country by train and by pony and trap, producing fine photographs of seaside resorts and beauty spots that were keenly bought by millions of Victorians. These prints were painstakingly pasted into family albums and pored over during the dark nights of winter, rekindling precious memories of summer excursions.

The Rise of Frith & Co

Frith's studio was soon supplying retail shops all over the country. To meet the demand he gathered about him a small team of photographers, and published the work of independent artist-photographers of the calibre of Roger Fenton and Francis Bedford. In order to gain some understanding of the scale of Frith's business one only has to look at the catalogue issued by Frith & Co in 1886: it runs to some 670 pages, listing not only many thousands of views of the British Isles but also many photographs of most European countries,

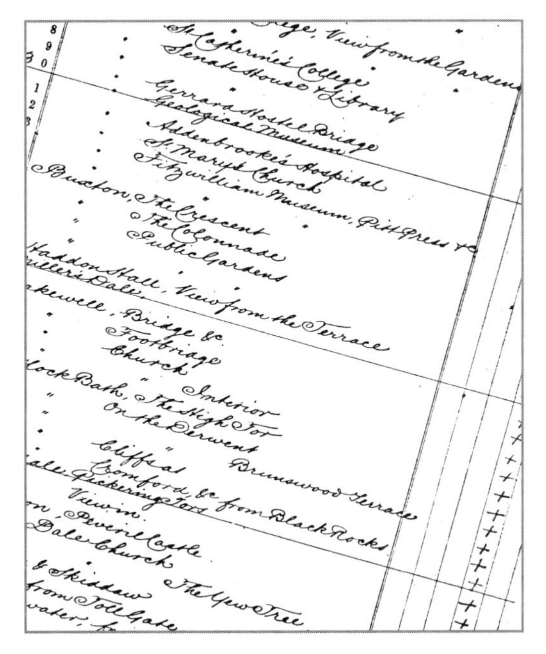
...ge, View from the Gardens
St Catherine's College
Senate House & Library
Geological Museum
Addenbrooke's Hospital
St Mary's Church
Fitzwilliam Museum, Pitt Press &c
Buxton, The Crescent
The Colonnade
Public Gardens
Haddon Hall, View from the Terrace
...kewell, Bridge &c.
Footbridge
Church
Interior
...ock Bath, The High Tor
On the Derwent
Cliffs at
Brunswood Terrace
Cromford, &c from Black Rocks
View in
...n, Peveril Castle
Dale Church
The Yew Tree
& Skiddaw
from Toll Gate

and China, Japan, the USA and Canada – note the sample page shown above from the hand-written *Frith & Co* ledgers detailing pictures taken. By 1890 Frith had created the greatest specialist photographic publishing company in the world, with over 2,000 outlets – more than the combined number that Boots and WH Smith have today! The picture on the right shows the *Frith & Co* display board at Ingleton in the Yorkshire Dales. Beautifully constructed with mahogany frame and gilt inserts, it could display up to a dozen local scenes.

Postcard Bonanza

The ever-popular holiday postcard we know today took many years to develop. In 1870 the Post Office issued the first plain cards, with a pre-printed stamp on one face. In 1894 they allowed other publishers' cards to be sent through the mail with an attached adhesive halfpenny stamp. Demand grew rapidly, and in 1895 a new size of postcard was permitted called the court card, but there was little room for illustration. In 1899, a year after Frith's death, a new card measuring 5.5 x 3.5 inches became the standard format, but it was not until 1902 that the divided back came into being, with address and message on one face and a full-size illustration on the other. *Frith & Co* were in the vanguard of postcard development, and Frith's sons Eustace and Cyril continued their father's monumental task, expanding the number of views offered to the public and recording more and more places in Britain, as the coasts and countryside were opened up to mass travel.

Francis Frith died in 1898 at his villa in Cannes, his great project still growing. The archive he created continued in business for another seventy years. By 1970 it contained over a third of a million pictures of 7,000 cities, towns and villages. The massive photographic record Frith has left to us stands as a living monument to a special and very remarkable man.

Frith's Archive: A Unique Legacy

FRANCIS FRITH'S legacy to us today is of immense significance and value, for the magnificent archive of evocative photographs he created provides a unique record of change in 7,000 cities, towns and villages throughout Britain over a century and more. Frith and his fellow studio photographers revisited locations many times down the years to update their views, compiling for us an enthralling and colourful pageant of British life and character.

We tend to think of Frith's sepia views of Britain as nostalgic, for most of us use them to conjure up memories of places in our own lives with which we have family associations. It often makes us forget that to Francis Frith they were records of daily life as it was actually being lived in the cities, towns and villages of his day. The Victorian age was one of great and often bewildering change for ordinary people, and though the pictures evoke an impression of slower times, life was as busy and hectic as it is today.

We are fortunate that Frith was a photographer of the people, dedicated to recording the minutiae of everyday life. For it is this sheer wealth of visual data, the painstaking chronicle of changes in dress, transport, street layouts, buildings, housing, engineering and landscape that captivates us so much today. His remarkable images offer us a powerful link with the past and with the lives of our ancestors.

See Frith at www.francisfrith.co.uk

Today's Technology

Computers have now made it possible for Frith's many thousands of images to be accessed almost instantly. In the Frith archive today, each photograph is carefully 'digitised' then stored on a CD Rom. Frith archivists can locate a single photograph amongst thousands within seconds. Views can be catalogued and sorted under a variety of categories of place and content to the immediate benefit of researchers.

Inexpensive reference prints can be created for them at the touch of a mouse button, and a wide range of books and other printed materials assembled and published for a wider, more general readership - in the next twelve months over a hundred Frith local history titles will be published! The day-to-day workings of the archive are very different from how they were in Francis Frith's time: imagine the herculean task of sorting through eleven tons of glass negatives as Frith had to do to locate a particular sequence of pictures! Yet the archive still prides itself on maintaining the same high standards of excellence laid down by Francis Frith, including the painstaking cataloguing and indexing of every view.

It is curious to reflect on how the internet now allows researchers in America and elsewhere greater instant access to the archive than Frith himself ever enjoyed. Many thousands of individual views can be called up on screen within seconds on one of the Frith internet sites, enabling people living continents away to revisit the streets of their ancestral home town, or view places in Britain where they have enjoyed holidays. Many overseas researchers welcome the chance to view special theme selections, such as transport, sports, costume and ancient monuments.

We are certain that Francis Frith would have heartily approved of these modern developments in imaging techniques, for he himself was always working at the very limits of Victorian photographic technology.

The Value of the Archive Today

Because of the benefits brought by the computer, Frith's images are increasingly studied by social historians, by researchers into genealogy and ancestory, by architects, town planners, and by teachers and schoolchildren involved in local history projects.

In addition, the archive offers every one of us an opportunity to examine the places where we and our families have lived and worked down the years. Highly successful in Frith's own era, the archive is now, a century and more on, entering a new phase of popularity.

The Past in Tune with the Future

Historians consider the Francis Frith Collection to be of prime national importance. It is the only archive of its kind remaining in private ownership and has been valued at a million pounds. However, this figure is now rapidly increasing as digital technology enables more and more people around the world to enjoy its benefits.

Francis Frith's archive is now housed in an historic timber barn in the beautiful village of Teffont in Wiltshire. Its founder would not recognize the archive office as it is today. In place of the many thousands of dusty boxes containing glass plate negatives and an all-pervading odour of photographic chemicals, there are now ranks of computer screens. He would be amazed to watch his images travelling round the world at unimaginable speeds through network and internet lines.

The archive's future is both bright and exciting. Francis Frith, with his unshakeable belief in making photographs available to the greatest number of people, would undoubtedly approve of what is being done today with his lifetime's work. His photographs, depicting our shared past, are now bringing pleasure and enlightenment to millions around the world a century and more after his death.

Berkshire Living Memories
An Introduction

SMALL THOUGH IT IS, Berkshire is packed with interest and steeped in history. With its gentle beauty and rich, varied landscape ranging from open downland with far-reaching views, woodlands and parks, to winding rivers and attractive villages, it is hardly surprising that visitors and residents alike are drawn to its numerous charms.

Berkshire really consists of two distinct parts. The western half is essentially rural and undeveloped - racing country. Here, the Lambourn Downs sweep down to the pretty river Lambourn, and the Berkshire Downs to the more majestic Thames, a river that surely, above all others, characterises the gentle, dignified beauty of England. Between the M4 and A4, near Newbury, there are areas of delightful woodland and common land where pretty villages nestle among the trees and open spaces.

The eastern half of Berkshire is quite different. Here, there is an awesome concentration of housing, as well as industrial and commercial development. In recent years towns like Slough, Maidenhead, Bracknell, Wokingham and Reading have encroached on the surrounding countryside, and now we have to look hard to find truly unspoilt pockets of peace and tranquillity. But they are there, providing refuge from the urban jungle, if we are prepared to look for them. The villages around Maidenhead and towards Henley are probably the best examples of areas which, so far, have been affected to a

lesser degree by town planners and developers.

But what of Berkshire's roots? To what extent have the county's characteristics influenced and shaped the landscape? How has it developed and evolved over the centuries, and what has it retained for today's generation? To find out, we need to embark on a journey within Berkshire's boundaries.

Stone Age, Bronze Age and Iron Age people all lived within the county and left their stamp on Berkshire. Burial mounds and Iron Age hillforts are scattered over the landscape, and Britain's oldest road, the Ridgeway, traces a line across open downland country above the Thames. Following the Roman invasion in AD 43, the town then known as Calleva Atrebatum, and now known as Silchester, was established just over the county boundary in Hampshire.

After the fall of the Roman Empire, Berkshire continued to attract attention. To begin with, the Saxons wrestled it from the Romano-Britons in the 6th century; then two Saxon kingdoms, Mercia and Wessex, battled for possession of it. Finally, the Danish Vikings raided it several times, firstly in AD 871.

The Normans made their presence felt, too. Many churches within the county contain fascinating examples of their work. In 1066 one man chose a chalk hill at the eastern end of the county to construct a fortress that would form part of a defensive ring round London: here, William the Conqueror built one of Berkshire's most prominent landmarks - Windsor Castle, which stands proudly above the Thames and gives the county its royal status.

Between the Middle Ages and the 17th century, Berkshire witnessed great activity in the wool and cloth trade. Newbury's historic St Nicolas's is Berkshire's 'wool church', built by John Winchcombe, a friend of kings and described as 'the richest clothier England ever beheld'. He began with nothing, but ended up with more than 200 looms. The church was started by Jack O'Newbury, as he was known, but finished in 1532 by his son.

It was about one hundred years later that one of the most important chapters in Newbury's history was written. At the time of the Civil War, Donnington Castle, to the north of the town, belonged to John Packer. His refusal of a loan to the King and opposition in Parliament led to the sequestration of his property by Charles I. Colonel John Boys was sent to take command of the castle for the King in September 1643, with 200 foot, 25 horse and four pieces of cannon. He strengthened the defences of the castle by constructing earthworks around it, which can still be seen today. He withstood two Parliamentary assaults on the castle in July and September 1644, and was knighted by the King in October 1644 before the second Battle of Newbury later that month.

This battle was somewhat inconclusive, but the Royalist Army was able to slip away leaving the Crown, the Great Seal, and the artillery in Boys' keeping at Donnington. Boys then withstood a siege by the Parliamentarians until he was relieved and provisioned by the King on 9 November. Repeated attempts were made to take the castle, but Boys did not surrender until he was instructed by the King to do so on 1 April 1646. The outline of the castle is still visible; the most impressive feature still standing is its splendid gatehouse, which can be seen from different parts of the town.

Agriculture has played its part in Berkshire's history. The county's farmers took a crucial role in the agricultural revolution of the 18th and early 19th centuries. Jethro Tull, who invented the seed drill and the horse-drawn hoe, will always be remembered as a pioneer of early agricultural development. He was born in 1674 and baptised in the church at Basildon, near Pangbourne. Ill-health forced him to give up an intended career in politics; he turned instead to farming, working on his inventions at Prosperous Farm, just outside Hungerford. However, his ideas were not well received by a suspicious and traditionalist farming establishment, and it was not until after his death in 1741 that the value of his work was finally acknowledged.

For the next one hundred and fifty years or so, the map of Berkshire gradually changed as canals, roads and railway lines threaded their way across the county. The age of transport had dawned at last. What we now know as the A4 was established as the Bath Road, its rough, rutted surface significantly improved by the introduction of turnpike trusts. Coaching inns began to appear along the route too, and towns and villages in the vicinity of the road grew in size and importance.

Running parallel to the Bath Road through Berkshire were two other lines of communication. Brunel's Great Western Railway marched cross-country towards Bristol, and the Kennet and Avon Canal, completed in 1810 at a cost of one million pounds, cut through the heart of West Berkshire.

Growth continued to influence the county, but it was the second half of the 20th century that witnessed even greater changes in Berkshire and the rest of the south-east of England. Traffic gradually became heavier, new roads and motorways began to spring up everywhere, and the population of the county increased dramatically as thousands of new homes were built within its boundaries.

Just before these changes began to make an impact, Francis Frith's expert team of photographers set their sights on Berkshire, capturing a way of life that has largely gone forever - and yet many of us still remember it with affection and nostalgia. Anyone who lived through the 1950s and 60s will recognise many of the photographs in this book, not necessarily every church, town, village or street, but the fashions and the cars and the well-ordered structure of our daily lives. Above all, Frith's images represent a fascinating social record of the time.

Around Ascot

Wellington College c1960 W46047
Wellington College, one of Britain's most famous public schools, dates back to the mid 19th century; it was founded as a memorial to the Duke of Wellington, following his splendid victory at Waterloo in 1815.

▼ **Sunninghill, The Three Jays c1955** S230007

The Three Jays at Sunninghill was damaged by fire in recent years, and was eventually razed to the ground to make way for a new residential development. Note the three jays on the Simonds inn sign.

▼ **Sunninghill, The Village c1960** S230003

Little has changed since the early 1960s when this photograph was taken. The greenery is a little thicker, the brand names have changed and there are more cars. Shell is now UK, and the bus stop can still be seen opposite. Note the mini in the picture, launched in the summer of 1959. The belfry is still clearly identifiable today, crowning the roof of the village hall, which was built in memory of Thomas Cordes who lived at nearby Silwood Park.

▲ **Sunningdale Chobham Road c1965**

S574084

The shopping parade on the right has a striking Gothic look to it. The telephone box is still in the same place today, though yellow lines restrict parking on the right-hand side of the road. The shops have changed, and Brown's the Post Office by the junction and Barton Wyatt next door to it have gone.

Sunningdale Coworth Road c1960

S574063

Coworth Stores has become an antique gallery and the Sunningdale Post Office is now the premises of a chartered surveyor. The telegraph pole on the right has been replaced and many of the houses have been whitewashed. Coworth Road lies in Sunningdale village, off the A30.

BARCLAYS BANK LIMITED
CAFE

Sunningdale Station Road c1955

S574024

Street lighting has been added since this photograph was taken. The coal depot on the right of the picture has been replaced by a branch of Waitrose, though the National Westminster Bank continues to trade. Barclays is also still on the left-hand side of the road, and the mock-Tudor building adjoining it is now an Indian restaurant. Judging by the angle, it looks as if this picture might have been taken from a passing train - the railway crosses the road at this point.

▼ **Sunningdale, London Road c1955** S574086
The kerb drops on the left of the picture remain, though the Garden Machine Centre has gone. Further down the road, by the junction with Chobham Road, is a striking fake lodge with a slate roof - the premises of an estate agent. The mock-Tudor gables on the corner remain.

▼ **Sandhurst, Wellington Road c1960** S56009
The village of Sandhurst witnessed extensive development in the second half of the 20th century, and these days it lies in the shadow of Bracknell, Farnborough and Camberley. Note the old black and white signpost pointing towards Crowthorne and Bracknell, and the familiar telephone box on the corner.

▲ **Sandhurst The Halt and Yorktown Road c1960** S56004
The entrance to the village railway station can be seen on the corner, close to the point where the road passes under the line. A few basic station buildings are visible at the top of the slope. Only a stone's throw from here lies the River Blackwater, forming the county boundary between Berkshire and Hampshire.

◄ **Sandhurst**
The Post Office c1955
S56001
The village Post Office can be seen in this photograph, with a familiar Wall's advertisement at the front of the premises. The name 'Sandhurst' is of Saxon origin: 'hurst' means 'a wooded eminence', and 'sand' refers to the type of soil. Sheep breeding was introduced locally during the reign of Henry VIII, and gradually the population began to increase.

Little Sandhurst, High Street c1960 L487029
This part of East Berkshire consists almost entirely of 19th-century development; here and there are a few large Victorian houses with huge plate-glass windows and free Renaissance decorations.

Ascot, High Street c1955 A64002
We can see two soldiers standing outside the local Post Office. Note the distinctive awning, helping to shade the window displays, and up above the shop fronts are large adverts for Hovis, and meat, fish, game, poultry and ice.

Ascot High Street c1960 A64075
Ascot, close to the Surrey border, now has a strong suburban feel to it, with an abundance of Edwardian villas and shop fronts. The village has grown and developed in the shadow of the famous racecourse, which occupies an elevated position overlooking the surrounding area. Close by lies Windsor Great Park.

◄ **Crowthorne Dukes Ride c1955** C199094
The name of Crowthorne takes its name from a group of thorn trees at nearby Brookers Corner. Originally, the name 'Albertonville' was suggested in honour of the Prince Consort.

Crowthorne, High Street c1955 C199013
The centre of Crowthorne dates back to about the 1860s, and by the time this picture was taken - almost one hundred years later - many shops had been established in the High Street. The Wellesley Stores on the corner, now displaying piles of tins in the window, was opened in 1866. On the right are Hovis and Wills's Gold Flake advertisements, and a classic Guinness poster.

Crowthorne, High Street c1955 C199002
Crowthorne has expanded in every direction over the years, with new housing estates and infilling springing up all over the place. However, the influence of the Roman occupation is still in evidence in the area. The Devil's Highway, a Roman road, passes through the village, and two Roman milestones can still be seen locally. The Crowthorne Inn and an Esso garage are just visible in the photograph.

Bracknell, The Old Manor Hotel c1955 B172010

Take a walk through Bracknell today and you would not recognise this photograph. The Old Manor Hotel remains, covered by creeper, but it now stands at one end of a walkway through the town centre which was redeveloped following the decision to expand Bracknell. In the nearby underpass, a set of murals depicts the old town before it changed for good.

Jacksons
SMITHS
COACH
BUILDERS
SHOE
REPAIRS
SRX 881

Bracknell
High Street c1965
B172048
With New Town status and under the aegis of the Development Corporation, Bracknell began to expand rapidly. The town's first factory was in production by 1952; by the time this photograph was taken, the population had quadrupled. On the right is the brick-built Post Office, and on the left are the premises of Smith's, the coach builders, and Frisby's shoeshop.

◄ **Harmans Water The Square c1965** H336002

Devastated by constant bombing, Britain's bigger cities faced acute housing shortages by the end of the Second World War. The answer seemed to lie in the development of new towns up and down the country. One of these new communities was Bracknell New Town, established to help relieve the housing crisis in West London. Harmans Water was the last of the original neighbourhoods to be built, and the first houses were occupied in 1961.

Easthampstead
The Church c1960 E144008
Dedicated in 1867, the church of St Michael and St Mary Magdalene includes a monument to John Delane, editor of the London Times. The wonderfully eye-catching east window depicts the Last Judgement, combining the work of William Morris and Edward Burne-Jones. The church is also associated with an amusing story. The local squire, the Marquis of Downshire, caught his hat on the branches of some trees in the churchyard. The vicar refused to trim them, and so the Marquis donated a clock to the local workhouse instead of the church. The clock can still be seen opposite.

Binfield
The Village c1955 B97005
The poet Alexander Pope lived at Binfield as a boy and sang in the local choir. His father made his fortune as a linen draper, and bought an imposing country house in Murrell Hill Lane in the village. The shop on the corner has an advertisement on the wall for Craven A - a once-famous and very popular brand of cigarettes.

Hawthorn Hill
Ruffs Orchard Donkey Stud c1960 H390303
This charming picture depicts a small boy sitting astride a patient donkey at Ruffs Orchard. The stud closed in the 1960s. Hawthorn Hill opened as a point to point course for local farmers and royal buckhounds in 1881. The military became associated with the course in 1900 when it was upgraded to National Hunt status. Later, in the 1940s, the site switched to pony and trap racing. Today, Hawthorn Hill is the setting for a golf course.

Around Windsor

Bisham
The National Recreational Centre c1955 B101011
Queen Victoria is said to have called here whilst out driving in her carriage, but found no-one at home. This photograph captures some gentle activity on the Thames, with the Tudor house, built by Sir Philip Hoby using fragments of the original abbey, on the far bank. The house is the setting for the Sports Council's National Recreation Centre.

Wraysbury, The Bells of Ouzeley c1965 W150022
Now a Harvester, the Bells of Ouzeley was Jerome K Jerome's 'picturesque inn' in 'Three Men in a Boat'. The bells are understood to be those of Osney Abbey in Oxford; in 1538 they were transported downstream by the monks in an attempt to prevent Henry VIII from seizing them. The barges went aground at Wraysbury, and the bells were apparently hidden in the oozing mud. They have never been found.

Wraysbury, High Street c1955 W150003
East of Old Windsor, Wraysbury was once part of Buckinghamshire. With neighbouring Horton, the village was absorbed into Berkshire in 1974 as part of the county boundary changes introduced that year. Wraysbury is by the Thames and close to several large reservoirs.

Wraysbury, The Village Sign c1955 W150009
This very striking village sign illustrates Wraysbury's connection with the Magna Carta. It was in 1215 that King John signed the historic charter, establishing the principle of constitutional monarchy and securing democracy, liberty and justice for all individuals. Runnymede remains an unspoilt meadow, much-loved by locals and tourists alike.

Windsor, The River c1960 W111065
One of Windsor's most famous views shows the town's bridge in the distance, which was erected in 1822. Until the 20th century, there was a toll - the living paid 2d, while the departed could be carried across by coffin for 6/8d! In the foreground are several pleasure boats - the 'Monarch I', the 'Humble' and the 'Angler'. Sir Christopher Wren's old home, now a hotel, stands on the right bank, near the bridge.

Windsor, Castle Hill c1960 W111093
At the bottom of this picture is the imposing statue of Queen Victoria, erected in 1887 for the Golden Jubilee to mark the 50th anniversary of her coronation. The statue stands on the site of an old market cross. A policeman stood here on traffic duty until the 1950s.

Windsor, The Castle c1955 W111029
Windsor Castle was founded as a fortress by William the Conqueror, and has been substantially altered and extended over the centuries. During his reign, George IV spent nearly one million pounds on improving this most historic of Berkshire landmarks. Windsor Castle's famous Round Tower, built by Henry II, can be seen on the right of the picture.

Windsor, The Castle, The Changing of the Guard c1960 W111309
Windsor Castle is the largest inhabited castle in the world and the oldest in continuous occupation. Originally constructed of earth and timber as part of a ring of defences around London, the castle was later rebuilt in stone. Following the restoration of the monarchy under Charles II, Windsor Castle evolved into the palace we know today.

WEY

Old Windsor
The Lock c1955

O130026

Old Windsor was described in the Domesday Book as the third largest town in Berkshire. The Saxon kings built a palace here, and it was during a visit to the area that William the Conqueror chose the site for the fortress we know today as Windsor Castle. As the new town evolved, so Old Windsor decreased in size to a small village. In this picture, passers-by and the lock-keeper watch a boat pass through the lock.

▼ **Old Windsor, The Landing Stage c1955** O130011
Old Windsor witnessed a good deal of residential development following the Second World War; today, this village is one of Berkshire's most expensive and sought-after addresses. Sir Christopher Wren represented Old Windsor as its Member of Parliament.

▼ **Maidenhead, The Town Hall c1960** M7072
This, the original Town Hall, stood on the corner of Park Street and the High Street. The present Town Hall, built in 1962, is nearby in St Ives Road and stands on the site of the Manor of Ive, part of the divorce settlement between Henry VIII and Anne of Cleves. Eagle-eyed movie buffs will recognise it as a hospital in some of the 'Carry On' films.

▲ **Maidenhead Boulter's Lock c1955** M7054
Boulter's Lock is probably the most famous lock on the Thames, and was the first and the lowest on the river of the first set of eight to be built under the legislation of 1770. The lock has always been a popular spot. A boulter was another name for a miller.

Maidenhead
The River Thames c1960
M7037
A bustling scene on the Thames. On the extreme right is Maidenhead Bridge, designed by Sir Robert Taylor and rebuilt in 1777. At the height of the coaching era, up to five hundred coaches crossed the bridge every day. Opposite is the Thames Riviera Hotel, and beside it is the town's rowing club.

CROWN
HOTEL
TOBACCONIST

Maidenhead Bridge Street c1955
M7016
Much of Bridge Street has changed over the years. The Crown Hotel, seen on the left, has gone. Traffic was lighter in the mid 1950s, as we can see. Bridge Street was originally a causeway across low-lying ground, and the town's ford once stood here.

▼ **Eton, Eton College, Jourdelay's c1955** E43032
Founded by Henry VI in 1440, Eton College was modelled on Winchester College, making it the second oldest public school in the country. Originally the school accommodated 70 poor scholars who were educated free of charge. The boys still wear black tail coats in mourning for George III, their favourite monarch.

▼ **Datchet, The Green c1965** D9125
On the left of the picture, overlooking the Green, stands the Royal Stag, once the home of Robert Barker, printer to Elizabeth I. The pub sign stands across the road. A couple of doors along is Edwards', the provision merchants. This photograph was taken before the M4 motorway traffic from London came along here en route to Windsor. The church spire of St Mary the Virgin surveys the scene.

▲ **Datchet**
The Green and the War Memorial c1955 D9026
About ten years before photograph D9125 was taken, the Royal Stag looked a little different. The inn sign can just be seen on the edge of the green. Clearly visible in the foreground is Datchet's War Memorial. To the right of it is the International Stores.

Datchet
The Green c1955 D9074
The Green at Datchet is more or less deserted in this picture. A single-decker bus waits at the bus stop, and several bicycles can be seen propped up at the kerb on the right of the photograph. Also on this side of the Green stands the Morning Star pub.

Datchet, High Street c1945 D9056

The old Baptist church on the far left is now three shops. The house next door is ornately decorated with a balcony; during the early part of the 20th century it became a butcher's shop. The oak tree in the middle of the picture was planted to commemorate Queen Victoria's Golden Jubilee in 1887. To the right of the tree is a branch of Barclays Bank, which closed some years ago. To the right of it is the Manor Hotel. Note the old AA logo on the sign at the front.

Datchet, High Street c1955 D9083

Striking Victorian and Edwardian villas can be seen lining Datchet High Street. The scene of Falstaff's miseries in Shakespeare's 'The Merry Wives of Windsor', Datchet stands on the Thames bank, opposite Home Park. One mile above the village, accompanied by the Provost of Eton College, the legendary angler Izaak Walton used to fish 'for a little samlet or skegger trout, and catch 20 or 40 of them at a standing'.

Datchet High Street c1955 D9011

A view of Datchet High Street from The Green. Just before the turn of the century, and again soon after the Second World War, Datchet suffered serious flooding when the swollen Thames caused a pond in the centre of the village to overflow. Several anxious residents were isolated in their homes.

◀ **Cookham**
High Street c1955 C157017
Cookham will always be associated with the artist Stanley Spencer who died in 1959, soon after this photograph was taken. Spencer was a controversial figure and even now, more than 40 years after his death, his work is the subject of speculation and debate.

RESTAURANT
BEL AND
THE DRAGON
HOTEL

Cookham
High Street c1955
C157032
The 17th-century Kings Arms Hotel is on the right of the street, while the Bell and the Dragon stands on the opposite side. A former Methodist chapel, located on the right-hand corner of the street by the junction, became the Stanley Spencer Gallery in 1962. Many of his paintings are exhibited inside. Spencer used the village as the background for much of his work.

Cookham Dean, The Jolly Farmer c1950 C353004
Thought to date back about 200 years, the Jolly Farmer was once the local mortuary. Back in the mid 1980s, the future of this delightful little inn was in doubt when the brewers Courage decided to dispose of it. Faced with the threat of closure, the regular customers formed a consortium and bought the inn in July 1987, ensuring its future for all who frequent it. The Courage sign, now long gone, can be seen on the sign above the door. Today, an enclosed porch, new windows and tables and benches at the front give the place a smarter look.

Bray, The Lock c1960 B191029
This picture was taken about ten years before the last stretch of the nearby M4 was finally completed. Famous for a ballad about a local vicar who frequently changed his religion to avoid losing his desirable living, Bray is regarded as one of the most attractive villages on the Thames.

Around Reading

Ruscombe
The Village c1960 R402032
Just visible on the left of this photograph is Ruscombe's Church of St James the Great. Made of flint, the chancel is all that is left of the original structure. The nave and tower were rebuilt in the 1860s. William Penn, who founded Pennsylvania, lived near the church until his death in 1718.

▼ **Waltham St Lawrence, The Village c1955** W377001

The Bell, one of Berkshire's loveliest and most historic inns, dates from the 14th century, though much of the existing building is early 16th-century. This is a pub with a fascinating history. During the Civil War, a small chamber enabled Parliamentarians to beat a hasty retreat through the pub's back entrance when Royalist forces were approaching. Built as a private house, the Bell passed to the village in the 17th century. These days it is administered by a charity and leased by the landlord.

▼ **Waltham St Lawrence, The Street c1955** W377013

Close to the old village Post Office stands a pound where animals were once tethered. At one time there was an August fair here, consisting of sideshows and many stalls. The church dates back to the 11th century, and evidence suggests that the Romans and the Saxons once occupied this site.

▲ **Wargrave High Street c1955** W25003

The riverside village of Wargrave is quiet, except at weekends and during the summer months. Then it comes to life with groups of tourists and boating enthusiasts. The origin of Wargrave has no connection with military cemeteries, as some people mistakenly believe. Instead, the name means 'grove by the weirs'.

Wargrave
High Street and the White Hart Hotel c1955 W25011
When Edith, the wife of Edward the Confessor, held the manor it was known as 'Weregrave'. The church dates from the First World War, replacing an earlier church which was destroyed by fire on Whit Sunday, 1914. It is thought that the fire was the work of a militant wing of the Suffragettes - they were angry because the vicar would not withdraw the word 'obey' from the marriage service.

Wargrave
The St George and Dragon Hotel c1955
W25010

St George and the dragon are depicted on the inn sign and the gable end. Note the AA and RAC signs on the front wall, and the elaborate floral displays above the two porches. The sign for the cocktail lounge is something of a rarity today, and the old telephone box on the right is a nostalgic reminder of how Britain's streets looked in those lean, post-war years.

◄ **Wargrave Marsh Lock c1960**
W25029
A ferry once crossed the Thames here, and near the village the Henley branch of Brunel's Great Western Railway crosses the river. Iron studs were placed along the meadow here in 1903 to define the 14-ft width of the towing path. Most of the studs have disappeared, indicating the extent of the river bank's erosion. In this picture, the 'Mary Kay' can be seen passing through the lock.

▼ **Sonning High Street c1955** S149046
Pronounced 'Sunning', the village of Sonning is full of charm and character. Once a palace of the Bishops of Salisbury, it was through Sonning's streets that Dick Turpin galloped after a hold-up on the nearby Bath Road. He apparently stabled his horse at his aunt's cottage in the village before going into hiding in neighbouring Oxfordshire until the dust settled.

◄ **Sonning The Village c1955** S149055
Many Georgian and timber-framed cottages line the streets of Sonning. Edward Hudson, the owner of 'Country Life', lived in the village in a house designed for him by Sir Edwin Lutyens in 1901.

Sonning, The Lock c1955 S149024
The Thames falls gently by 4 ft at Sonning Lock. A short distance from here, the river is crossed by a bridge which is understood to be the oldest on the Thames. Colourful flower beds and borders line the banks, and, being a fine day, it is not surprising that the towpath attracts large numbers of people.

Sonning, The Bridge and the White Hart Hotel c1955 S149005
The oldest part of the hotel dates back to the Elizabethan era, when it was a hostelry for those passing by on the river. Its name comes from the white hart on the coat of arms of Richard II, whose queen, Isabella of France, was imprisoned in the Bishop's Palace, later destroyed by Cromwell and his men. To the right of the hotel is Sonning's redbrick 18th-century bridge.

Sonning, The River and the French Horn Hotel c1960 S149074

The French Horn Hotel dates back to the 1880s, and was built on the site of an older inn which overlooked the Thames at Sonning Eye. The hotel continues to trade today. American and Canadian troops were billeted in Sonning before the D-Day landings, and General Eisenhower stayed briefly in the village. The playwright Terence Rattigan lived at Sonning for several years after the Second World War.

Twyford, London Road c1955 T331022

We can see several pubs in this photograph of Twyford, a sprawling commuter village between Reading and Maidenhead. The Royal Oak is on the far right of the picture, and further down stands the King's Arms Hotel. Across the road we can just pick out the village Post Office.

◄ **Twyford High Street c1955**

T331006

The Duke of Wellington pub and the Post Office stand some way down the street, while the premises of W Barrett & Sons, the butchers, can be seen just beyond the parked car on the left. Twyford became an ecclesiastical parish in 1876 when it was separated from the smaller village of Hurst.

◀ **Twyford**
High Street c1955
T331011
Look for the Hovis signs on the right-hand side of the road, one almost concealed by thick foliage. On the left is the Duke of Wellington, part of the Henley Brewery. According to a War Office document of 1686, there were 21 stablings and 29 beds in public houses in Twyford.

▼ **Twyford**
Waltham Road c1955
T331018
This picture of Twyford shows the Golden Cross on the Waltham Road, a Wethereds pub offering bed and breakfast, snacks and grills. Coach parties are welcome, as the sign indicates. Just down the street is an Esso garage.

◀ **Twyford**
Church Street c1955
T331004
The striking pub sign for the King's Arms can just be seen on the far left of the picture, and just below it is the sign for the National Provincial Bank, now defunct. On the opposite corner are the premises of C H Patrick, the chemist. The window is well stocked.

Finchampstead, The Queen's Oak Tree c1955 F26003
On the left of the picture, enclosed by creeper, is a plaque which reads: 'The oak tree near this stone was planted 21 June 1887 in commemoration of Queen Victoria's completion of the 50th year of her reign'. The stone was placed here in June 1897 to commemorate her Diamond Jubilee. To the right of it is a pub, the Queen's Oak, previously known as the White Horse; it probably dates back to the 18th century. The inn, now whitewashed, is a listed building.

Wokingham, Reading Road c1965 W123179
Wokingham was founded in the early 13th century by the Norman-French bishop, Roger le Poore. Until the 19th century the town expanded at a slow pace, but today Wokingham is a fast-growing community with easy and direct access to London, making it an obvious choice for commuters to live.

Wokingham, The Tudor House c1955 W123001
Dating back to the mid 16th century, the Tudor House is one of Wokingham's most historic and attractive buildings. Some of the windows retain their original ironwork. The front was partly altered in the early part of the 20th century by incorporating a small number of timbers from a nearby dismantled mansion. Until the end of the First World War, the building housed a school.

Wokingham, The Town Hall from the Market Place c1955 W123017
At one time a Guildhall stood on this site, which was built about the turn of the 17th century. The present triangular building dates back to 1860, and was designed in the Gothic revival style. Originally, the Town Hall was a police station, a court room and gaol. If you stand outside and look closely, you can spot 'County Police Station' inscribed in stone near the top of the building.

Wokingham Rose Street c1955

W123014

Just a stone's throw from the Town Hall lies Rose Street, full of charm and character and the finest example in Berkshire of a medieval 'enclosed' street. Founded by the Dean of Salisbury in the early 13th century, Rose Street is extremely wide at one end but narrow at the other. We can see a coal lorry towards the end of the street, and beyond it is the town's All Saints Church, enlarged in the 12th century and dedicated to All Saints by the Bishop of Salisbury in about 1193.

Wokingham
Fun at Lakeside Holidays, California c1960
W123077
Once part of the ancient Windsor Forest, the area now covered by this country park was cleared after the First World War and became the s of a holiday camp known as California-in-England. Part of the park, an area of woodland known as Vermont, also creat the impression that you migh be far from home.

◄ **Wokingham Denmark Street c1955**
W123016
Denmark Street, running south-west from the Market Place, has changed quite significantly since this photograph was taken, but in places there are still reminders of old Wokingham. Many of the houses in Denmark Street were built in the 15th, 16th or 17th century.

▼ **Wokingham Fun at Lakeside Holidays, California c1960** W123076
The holiday camp may have gone, but the lake continues to draw visitors here. Gentle walks and strolls by the lake shore make this one of the area's most popular country parks. Habitats here include heathland and woodland; the park is both a local nature reserve and a Site of Special Scientific Interest.

◄ **Winnersh The Church of St Mary the Virgin c1965**
W331038
The church in this photograph was newly-built when it was captured for posterity in the mid 1960s. The foundation stone was laid on 27 June 1965 by the Right Reverend Eric Knell, the Lord Bishop of Reading.

Winnersh, Sindlesham Mill c1960 W331029
At the time this photograph was taken, Winnersh and neighbouring Sindlesham were quiet villages to the south of Reading. Today, they lie in the shadow of the town, bisected by the M4. Sindlesham Mill is mentioned in the Domesday Book and is still standing today, just to the north of the motorway.

Tilehurst, The Triangle c1955 T48020
The War Memorial stands prominently by the Triangle in Tilehurst. The overhead wires enabled Reading's trolley buses to travel the town's streets and thoroughfares. On the right is the Plough Inn.

Tilehurst The Bear c1955 T48010
The Bear can be seen on the corner of Park Lane. Just beyond it is the distinctive water tower, constructed in 1931-32. The water tower is one of Reading's most famous landmarks; it can be seen from miles around. The Bear remains in business today.

Reading
Friar Street c1965 R13076
Friar Street in Reading's bustling town centre. Many of the shops and offices have changed hands since this picture was taken. The Post Office on the right has moved to the nearby Market Place.

NK

Reading
Broad Street c1965

R13085

Many of the shops in Broad Street have disappeared since this photograph was taken, though Marks and Spencer remains on the left. Broad Street is traffic free now; this is the main reason why Broad Street looks so different today.

Reading, The Town Hall c1955 R13024
Berkshire's county town is where Jane Austen went to school and Oscar Wilde was imprisoned. The town's industrial heritage is recorded in the local museum, and the remains of Reading Abbey, founded in 1121 by King Henry Beauclerc, can still be seen. The town's tourist information centre is located on the ground floor of the old Town Hall.

Reading, Caversham Bridge c1955 R13048
One of Reading's more familiar landmarks, Caversham Bridge connects the town centre with Caversham and Henley. Partly visible through the arches is Piper's Island, named after the local ferryman who lived there. The original bridge played a key role in the Civil War with Charles I and Prince Rupert engaged in a fierce fight here against the Earl of Essex.

Caversham, The River c1955 C52004
The Thames is one of the most important rivers in Britain; this stretch of it is particularly popular, cutting through some of the finest scenery in the south of England. Boat trips are also a regular activity here, enabling passengers to appreciate the river's beauty and unique character.

Caversham, Christchurch Meadows c1960 C52016
Christchurch Meadows look much the same today as they did in the 1950s. This photograph was taken from Reading Bridge, looking across to the north bank of the Thames.

Caversham, The Bridge c1955 C52008
Swans can be seen gliding on the waters of the Thames. Visitors to the riverbank often find large numbers of swans in the water or in the vicinity of the towpath. A cabin cruiser can be seen heading in their direction.

Purley, The Village c1955 P373002
Groups of picturesque red brick cottages convey the image of a sleepy village where very little happened. It is hard to believe from looking at the picture that Purley is now a residential suburb of Reading, with modern housing estates spreading in all directions. Until 1900, the population of Purley was less than two hundred.

Pangbourne High Street c1955 P5013
This photograph of Pangbourne was taken from the bridge over the Pang. The river rises on the Berkshire Downs, beginning as an intermittent chalk 'winterbourne' before maturing to a clear trout stream. Many varieties of plant grow in profusion along its banks.

Pangbourne
The George Hotel c1955
P5012

Two policemen on bicycles can be seen outside the George Hotel, which still trades in the village today. Long before this photograph was taken, Pangbourne established itself as a popular haunt of artists, writers and weekend anglers. D H Lawrence and his wife rented a cottage in the village in 1919.

Pangbourne, The Square c1955 P5100
This view of Pangbourne shows the bridge over the Pang, a tributary of the Thames. The scene looks much the same today - the centre of this pleasant riverside village has changed little over the years. The supermarket chain David Greig has gone.

Pangbourne, The Weir from Swan Yard c1955 P5043
The 17th-century Swan, on the outskirts of Pangbourne, is where Kenneth Grahame reputedly wrote most of his classic children's story 'The Wind in the Willows'. At one time the county boundary between Oxfordshire and Berkshire ran right through the middle of this building, dividing the two bars. The licensing laws differed either side of the line and closing time would vary by as much as half an hour. Keen drinkers simply moved from one county to the other by taking their drink into the other bar.

Stratfield Mortimer, The Village c1955 S821001
Stratfield Mortimer lies close to the Hampshire border and is joined almost imperceptibly with its neighbouring village of Mortimer. Nearby is the Devil's Highway, a Roman road running from London to Silchester. The road entered Berkshire near Bagshot and then followed a straight course as far as the east gate of the Roman town of Calleva Atrebatum, now known as Silchester.

Theale, Englefield House, The Terrace c1955 T254016
The house dates from the reign of Elizabeth I, but was largely rebuilt following a major fire which undermined the structure in 1886. It is difficult to say how much of the original Elizabethan work remains. The entrance tower on the east front is Victorian.

Englefield, The House and the Lake c1955 E145012
Cranemoor Lake stands in the foreground, with the outline of Englefield House in the distance, set against a curtain of woodland. Cedar trees on the right enhance the classic parkland scene. Englefield House is privately owned and not open to the public.

Theale, The Green c1955 T254006
Theale, near Reading, still has the air of a village about it, even though it has expanded enormously over the years. This photograph shows the western end of the village, in the days when the A4 London to Bath road ran through its centre.

Theale, High Street c1955 T254001
Much of Theale High Street remains unchanged, though it is unlikely that we would find this part of the village free of traffic today. The High Street was once a coaching route from London to Bath; these days, Theale by-pass keeps traffic out of the village. Items of historical interest, including tools and pottery, were found locally, suggesting there has been a settlement here since the early Iron Age.

Bradfield, The Greek Theatre c1960 B626009
Hidden away deep in a disused chalkpit below the road lies the Greek Theatre, part of Bradfield College. One of Britain's most famous public schools, Bradfield was founded by Thomas Stevens, the local vicar, in 1850.

Mortimer Common Victoria Road c1955

M322012

The Victoria Arms continues to trade as a pub. Although the exterior appearance of the inn is the same, the building is now adorned with hanging baskets and floral displays. The pub sign is also new. The cottage just beyond the Victoria Arms remains intact. Note the coach, possibly a school bus, parked at the side of the road.

▼ **Mortimer Common, West End Road c1955** M322038
The tower of the church of St John the Evangelist peeps through the trees at the far end of the road. The shops on the right have all changed hands since the 1950s, and the Shell BP garage has also gone.

▼ **Mortimer Common, Victoria Road and the Post Office c1955** M322007
The house on the left, partly obscured by trees, has new windows now, and the road in front of it has been widened since the 1950s. Opposite the junction, by the parked car, is one of the entrances to some playing fields.

▲ **Woolhampton The Row Barge Inn c1965** W376073
The inn has retained its charm and character over the years, and there have been only a few minor external changes since this photograph was taken. Coaching lamps and flower-filled hanging baskets adorn the walls, creating a delightfully colourful scene. Edward VII used to call here after spending the day at Newbury races.

Woolhampton
The Village c1965

W376022

Woolhampton lies on the A4 between Reading and Newbury. The shop on the right is still there, and so is the distinctive News sign on the end wall. For many years this shop was run by two brothers who decided to start their own business when they were demobbed after the Second World War. I lived in this village as a child, and often called into the shop for sweets!

Woolhampton, Station Road c1965 W376047
On the corner of Station Road is an enclosed drinking fountain inscribed with the words 'Righteousness Exalteth a Nation'. The fountain was built to mark Queen Victoria's Diamond Jubilee in 1897. The tall tower further along the street is part of a private house. Hobbs General Stores on the right has closed.

Woolhampton, The Village c1965 W376016
The Newspaper Shop, on the left, is now Woolhampton Stores and Newsagents, and the Angel Inn next door looks very different today, almost completely covered by ivy. There has been a pub on this site since 1752. The Old Bakery adjacent to it is now a private house.

Around Newbury

Newbury
Northbrook Street c1960 N61095
One of Newbury's most attractive streets, depicted at the beginning of the 1960s, Northbrook Street is noted for its mid to late Georgian buildings, and distinctive pink and blue brick houses above lines of modern shop fronts. Many familiar High Street stores lined the town's main thoroughfare, including Hepworths, Freeman Hardy and Willis and the International Stores.

NTIQUES
The Tudor Café
RAC
MILWARDS
103 Tudor Café 103
THE ANCHOR
SIMONDS
FRANKS

Newbury Northbrook Street 1954 N61041

On the left of the picture is the handsome façade of the Tudor Cafe; just beyond it is the Anchor pub, now a building society. To the right is Camp Hopson department store, with its rubbed brickwork, Doric and Ionic pilasters, and tile-hung gables. The store was established in 1921.

▼ **Newbury, The Broadway c1960** N61089
Before the A34 ring road, and long before the newly-opened Newbury bypass, through traffic travelled along Oxford Road, passing the Chequers Hotel which can be seen in the picture. Some of the buildings in The Broadway have Georgian fronts, while others date from the Queen Anne period.

▼ **Newbury, The Clock Tower from Oxford Road c1955** N61036
The clock tower, partly enclosed by an octagonal shelter and situated at the centre of a traffic system, stands on the site of a wayside chapel, disused in the 16th century, converted into houses and eventually demolished in 1791. Famous for its exposed ironwork, the clock tower has four illuminated dials and two drinking fountains; it cost £278 5s, which was subscribed by the townspeople.

▲ **Newbury Market Place c1960**
N61084
Beynons, Edwards and Godding and WJ Daniel & Co have all closed, though the Town Hall and its famous clock tower still remain. One of Newbury's most striking landmarks, the tower was completed in 1881. On the corner is a sign which prohibits the use of traction engines.

Newbury
The Jacobean Cloth Museum c1955 N61049
One of Newbury's most beautiful buildings, the Cloth Hall was restored in 1902, more than fifty years before this photograph was taken, in memory of Queen Victoria. Built in the 17th century to provide unemployed weavers with work, it was handed to the Corporation and later opened as the Town Museum.

Newbury
The Weavers' Cottages c1955
N61028
This delightful stretch of towpath, with its lines of quaint cottages and period houses, is where the Kennet & Avon Canal enters Newbury on its way to meet the Thames at Reading. These brick and timber-framed cottages are Jacobean, and the tile-hung east gable, partly visible on the extreme left, has moulded bargeboards and a picturesque oriel window which retains its old casements and leaded lights.

Newbury, Donnington Castle c1955 N61008

On a hillside near Newbury are the remains of Donnington Castle, once a vital stronghold commanding the key trade routes passing through the town. Its strategic importance was immense, as was borne out by the prolonged fight for it during the Civil War. The most impressive feature still standing is the castle's magnificent gatehouse.

Newbury, Victoria Park c1955 N61027
Victoria Park lies to the east of the town centre. Covering an area of seventeen acres, the park includes a statue of Queen Victoria guarded by two terracotta lions, which originally stood in the Market Place.

Thatcham, The Broadway c1955 T222005
Thatcham has grown and expanded enormously in recent years, though the character of the village centre remains intact. A flourishing market was once held here, though in the 12th century it was sabotaged by Newbury traders who were jealous of its success.

Thatcham, The Broadway c1955 T222017

The war memorial at the centre of Thatcham Broadway has been removed, and now most of the middle part of the road is taken up with parking spaces. As with most other towns and villages today, traffic has increased hugely; the streets of Thatcham are often clogged with motorists looking for a parking space.

Thatcham, The War Memorial c1955 T222006

The gabled building immediately to the left of the war memorial has survived the transformation of the village, though the shops to the right of it have been replaced by a modern shopping centre. Opposite the bus and the tree stands the King's Head, one of Thatcham's old coaching inns. Its owner feared significant loss of trade with the coming of the railways. She was an influential local landowner, and insisted that the railway be built well away from the village centre.

Thatcham High Street c1955 T222002

The little cottages between the first two parked cars have gone, and the Crown Inn on the right disappeared some years ago. Broadway Motor Works is now a car showroom.

Thatcham High Street c1960 T222040

The White Hart on the left still survives, with a similar pub sign. Oakeley Store on the right is now the premises of a photographer, and today the adjoining seed and agricultural merchants is an estate agent. In the 1950s and 60s the High Street accommodated two-way traffic. Today it is a one-way street with limited on-street parking.

Thatcham, Thatched Cottages c1955 T222041
These cottages were whitewashed and rethatched after a fire in the early 1970s. The house at right angles to the road is still there, though the lean-to with the slate roof has gone.

Hampstead Norris, The Village from Folly Hill c1960 H149002
Little has changed since this classic view of Hampstead Norreys and the surrounding countryside was captured by a photographer. During the Second World War, this hilltop was the site of an airfield, with Wellington bombers based here.

Hampstead Norris, Newbury Hill 1950 H149007
When this photograph was taken, there would have been a railway line running through the village, just yards from this cottage. The Didcot to Southampton railway eventually closed in 1964. The fencing on the left has been replaced by a brick and flint wall, and the cottage is still neatly thatched.

Hampstead Norris, The Village Centre c1950 H149009
The telephone box is still here on this stretch of road. Just around the corner stands the parish well, which was presented to the village by a resident of nearby Hawkridge in 1903. The well, no longer in use, stands beneath a tiled roof enclosed by wooden palings. The iron machinery for raising water is still intact.

LYONS CAKES
ESSO BLUE
SRX 477

Hermitage
The Post Office
and Hermitage Road
c1955 H335020

The shop on the right is Hermitage Post Office and Stores. Today the speed limit through the village is thirty miles per hour, not forty. Lyons Cakes and Brooke Bond Tea are among the items advertised outside the shop. Note the cars of the period, including the Jaguar parked at the side of the building.

Hermitage, The Fox Inn c1955 H335009
The Fox is still in business today - one of two pubs in Hermitage. Today, the inn sign depicts a fox rather than merely the name of the pub. As expected, the village signs have all been updated.

Hermitage, The Post Office and Hermitage Road c1955 H335010
D H Lawrence and his wife Frieda lived in Hermitage between 1917 and 1919. As Lawrence was a pacifist married to a German, it was important that they spent the last years of the First World War living quietly and discreetly in the countryside. But even in Hermitage they were not left in peace. Lawrence and his wife received many visits from the police.

Yattendon The Square and the Old Elm Tree c1965 Y32003
Since this photograph was taken in the mid 1960s, Yattendon's famous elm tree has gone, killed off by Dutch elm disease in the 1970s. An oak now stands on this site, planted in 1977 to mark the 25th anniversary of the reign of Queen Elizabeth II. The village shop to the left of the tree has been refurbished, and the cottages to the right of it remain just as picturesque today.

Yattendon
The Royal Oak and the Old Well c1965 Y32026
One of Berkshire's loveliest pubs, the Royal Oak, can be seen on the right of the picture. According to records, Oliver Cromwell and his Roundheads enjoyed a 'fynne' dinner at this 16th-century coaching inn, and then spent the night here before doing battle at Newbury.

Yattendon, The Square, Old Cottages and the Old Well c1965 Y32021
From the Royal Oak, the view through the camera lens would capture Yattendon's charming square, with the village shop visible in the corner. Yattendon is one of Berkshire's loveliest villages and it was here that the poet Robert Bridges lived for twenty two years. The well in the foreground later became the village bus shelter.

West Ilsley, The Harrow c1960 W549050
Little has changed here over the years. The Harrow pub sign can now be seen on the wall above the seat and the ground floor windows. On a glorious summer's afternoon, when there is a cricket match in progress on the green opposite the inn, the Harrow captures the essence of the classic English village.

West Ilsley, High Street c1955 W549013
Half hidden among the rolling expanses of the Berkshire Downs, West Ilsley has strong links with the horse racing world. Hardly surprising, considering the village has been home to many famous winners over the years, including Dunfermline, who won the Oaks and the St Leger in 1977.

West Ilsley, The Village c1955 W549007
Close to the village runs the Ridgeway, Britain's oldest road. Walkers who descend on West Ilsley would find the baker's ovens no longer in use and the blacksmith's shop long gone. The school closed in 1966.

Chieveley, The Manor and the Church c1955 C443025
Another of Berkshire's prettiest villages, Chieveley takes its name from the wild chives growing locally. Along the main street is the Manor House, with delightful views over the surrounding countryside. Cromwell's men camped nearby during the Civil War.

Streatley, High Street c1955 S221009
One of Berkshire's prettiest and most famous villages, Streatley looks across the Thames to Goring, its Oxfordshire neighbour. This picture shows the road, lined with charming houses and cottages, leading down from the Bull inn to the river bridge. The ivy-covered cottage on the right is now whitewashed and the creeper has been removed.

Streatley, The Bull Hotel c1955 S221021
The Bull at Streatley stands beside a busy road junction, though it was a good deal quieter when this photograph was taken. The pub was once a coaching inn for the Royal Mail coach to Oxford. Early in the 20th century, much of Streatley was owned by the famous Morrell brewing family. The main characters in Jerome K Jerome's 'Three Men in a Boat' visited the inn, which still boasts a post box and a water pump at the front.

Streatley
The Bull Saloon Bar
c1955 S221022
The inside of this quaint old inn looks a little different today, but when this photograph was taken, the Bull epitomised traditional unspoiled country pubs. In those days, the saloon bar assumed the look of someone's cosy living room, with chairs arranged on either side of the fireplace and bric-a-brac cluttering the walls.

Streatley, The Swan Inn c1955 S221007
The building at the centre of the photograph remains intact, though it has been extended on both sides. The riverbank has also been built up, with a raised terrace replacing the lawns. Trees partially obscure the crenellated church tower. The hotel is now known as the Swan Diplomat.

Streatley, The Weir c1955 S221003
The central part of the weir has been replaced with an access bridge, and the house on the far bank has new windows. The thickness of the trees and the vegetation makes this view of the Thames at Streatley harder to find today. The best vantage point is the busy road bridge linking Streatley and Goring, though there is no pavement on the east side.

Around Hungerford

Hungerford
Eddington c1965 H134089
The Red Lion on the right is now a restaurant and bar, while the café on the left is an antique shop - one of many in Hungerford. The Bear Hotel, one of Berkshire's most famous coaching inns, is where Samuel Pepys once stayed and ate 'very good troutes, eels and crayfish'. Twenty years later, in 1688, William of Orange accepted the throne of England here.

NDSOR & NEATE
NEWBURY

Hungerford High Street c1955
H134049
This photograph of Hungerford High Street depicts the ornately-decorated Victorian Town Hall just beyond the railway bridge. Many of the Georgian houses and shops are built in the red and blue brick so typical of Berkshire.

Hungerford, The Kennet and Avon Canal and Dunn Mill c1955 H134018
Dunn Mill is now largely concealed by willow trees growing on the canal bank. This is one of the prettiest stretches of the Kennet and Avon, and the scene has hardly changed at all in the intervening years.

Hungerford, The Canal c1955 H134082
Just the other side of Town Bridge in the centre of Hungerford is the site of the old Hungerford Wharf. This is where Russian tallow, the first commercial cargo, arrived in 1798. Today, picturesque cottages overlook the canal. In this photograph two young canoeists can be seen progressing along the waterway.

HALT
AT
MAJOR
ROAD
AHEAD

Lambourn High Street c1960

L530020

Until about one hundred years ago, there was a market in Lambourn. In those days the village was known as Chipping Lambourn - 'chipping' is an old English word for market and was once in common usage. The name Lambourn probably originates from the time when sheep on the nearby downs were dipped in the local stream or bourne.

LIBRARY
BANK

Lambourn
High Street c1960
L530019
The shop on the right has been converted to a private house, while the Methodist Chapel on the left is now offices. The Lloyds Bank branch has also gone. Lambourn churchyard contains the tombs of two dishonourable figures. One of them was the last man to be hanged for arson in Britain, while the other man was caught stealing sheep in the area.

Kintbury, The Kennet and Avon Canal c1965 K121002
Named after Charles Dundas, Baron Amesbury and the first chairman of the Kennet and Avon Canal Company, the Dundas Arms was built for local canal workers. It has been a pub for over 200 years and looks much the same today as it did when this photograph was taken. Customers like to sit outside in summer and enjoy the tranquil scene.

Index

Frith Book Co Titles

www.francisfrith.co.uk

The Frith Book Company publishes over 100 new titles each year. A selection of those currently available are listed below. For latest catalogue please contact Frith Book Co.

Town Books 96 pages, approx 100 photos. County and Themed Books 128 pages, approx 150 photos (unless specified). All titles hardback laminated case and jacket except those indicated pb (paperback)

Title	ISBN	Price
Amersham, Chesham & Rickmansworth (pb)	1-85937-340-2	£9.99
Ancient Monuments & Stone Circles	1-85937-143-4	£17.99
Aylesbury (pb)	1-85937-227-9	£9.99
Bakewell	1-85937-113-2	£12.99
Barnstaple (pb)	1-85937-300-3	£9.99
Bath (pb)	1-85937-419-0	£9.99
Bedford (pb)	1-85937-205-8	£9.99
Berkshire (pb)	1-85937-191-4	£9.99
Berkshire Churches	1-85937-170-1	£17.99
Blackpool (pb)	1-85937-382-8	£9.99
Bognor Regis (pb)	1-85937-431-x	£9.99
Bournemouth	1-85937-067-5	£12.99
Bradford (pb)	1-85937-204-x	£9.99
Brighton & Hove(pb)	1-85937-192-2	£8.99
Bristol (pb)	1-85937-264-3	£9.99
British Life A Century Ago (pb)	1-85937-213-9	£9.99
Buckinghamshire (pb)	1-85937-200-7	£9.99
Camberley (pb)	1-85937-222-8	£9.99
Cambridge (pb)	1-85937-422-0	£9.99
Cambridgeshire (pb)	1-85937-420-4	£9.99
Canals & Waterways (pb)	1-85937-291-0	£9.99
Canterbury Cathedral (pb)	1-85937-179-5	£9.99
Cardiff (pb)	1-85937-093-4	£9.99
Carmarthenshire	1-85937-216-3	£14.99
Chelmsford (pb)	1-85937-310-0	£9.99
Cheltenham (pb)	1-85937-095-0	£9.99
Cheshire (pb)	1-85937-271-6	£9.99
Chester	1-85937-090-x	£12.99
Chesterfield	1-85937-378-x	£9.99
Chichester (pb)	1-85937-228-7	£9.99
Colchester (pb)	1-85937-188-4	£8.99
Cornish Coast	1-85937-163-9	£14.99
Cornwall (pb)	1-85937-229-5	£9.99
Cornwall Living Memories	1-85937-248-1	£14.99
Cotswolds (pb)	1-85937-230-9	£9.99
Cotswolds Living Memories	1-85937-255-4	£14.99
County Durham	1-85937-123-x	£14.99
Croydon Living Memories	1-85937-162-0	£9.99
Cumbria	1-85937-101-9	£14.99
Dartmoor	1-85937-145-0	£14.99
Derby (pb)	1-85937-367-4	£9.99
Derbyshire (pb)	1-85937-196-5	£9.99
Devon (pb)	1-85937-297-x	£9.99
Dorset (pb)	1-85937-269-4	£9.99
Dorset Churches	1-85937-172-8	£17.99
Dorset Coast (pb)	1-85937-299-6	£9.99
Dorset Living Memories	1-85937-210-4	£14.99
Down the Severn	1-85937-118-3	£14.99
Down the Thames (pb)	1-85937-278-3	£9.99
Down the Trent	1-85937-311-9	£14.99
Dublin (pb)	1-85937-231-7	£9.99
East Anglia (pb)	1-85937-265-1	£9.99
East London	1-85937-080-2	£14.99
East Sussex	1-85937-130-2	£14.99
Eastbourne	1-85937-061-6	£12.99
Edinburgh (pb)	1-85937-193-0	£8.99
England in the 1880s	1-85937-331-3	£17.99
English Castles (pb)	1-85937-434-4	£9.99
English Country Houses	1-85937-161-2	£17.99
Essex (pb)	1-85937-270-8	£9.99
Exeter	1-85937-126-4	£12.99
Exmoor	1-85937-132-9	£14.99
Falmouth	1-85937-066-7	£12.99
Folkestone (pb)	1-85937-124-8	£9.99
Glasgow (pb)	1-85937-190-6	£9.99
Gloucestershire	1-85937-102-7	£14.99
Great Yarmouth (pb)	1-85937-426-3	£9.99
Greater Manchester (pb)	1-85937-266-x	£9.99
Guildford (pb)	1-85937-410-7	£9.99
Hampshire (pb)	1-85937-279-1	£9.99
Hampshire Churches (pb)	1-85937-207-4	£9.99
Harrogate	1-85937-423-9	£9.99
Hastings & Bexhill (pb)	1-85937-131-0	£9.99
Heart of Lancashire (pb)	1-85937-197-3	£9.99
Helston (pb)	1-85937-214-7	£9.99
Hereford (pb)	1-85937-175-2	£9.99
Herefordshire	1-85937-174-4	£14.99
Hertfordshire (pb)	1-85937-247-3	£9.99
Horsham (pb)	1-85937-432-8	£9.99
Humberside	1-85937-215-5	£14.99
Hythe, Romney Marsh & Ashford	1-85937-256-2	£9.99

Available from your local bookshop or from the publisher

Frith Book Co Titles (continued)

Title	ISBN	Price
Ipswich (pb)	1-85937-424-7	£9.99
Ireland (pb)	1-85937-181-7	£9.99
Isle of Man (pb)	1-85937-268-6	£9.99
Isles of Scilly	1-85937-136-1	£14.99
Isle of Wight (pb)	1-85937-429-8	£9.99
Isle of Wight Living Memories	1-85937-304-6	£14.99
Kent (pb)	1-85937-189-2	£9.99
Kent Living Memories	1-85937-125-6	£14.99
Lake District (pb)	1-85937-275-9	£9.99
Lancaster, Morecambe & Heysham (pb)	1-85937-233-3	£9.99
Leeds (pb)	1-85937-202-3	£9.99
Leicester	1-85937-073-x	£12.99
Leicestershire (pb)	1-85937-185-x	£9.99
Lincolnshire (pb)	1-85937-433-6	£9.99
Liverpool & Merseyside (pb)	1-85937-234-1	£9.99
London (pb)	1-85937-183-3	£9.99
Ludlow (pb)	1-85937-176-0	£9.99
Luton (pb)	1-85937-235-x	£9.99
Maidstone	1-85937-056-x	£14.99
Manchester (pb)	1-85937-198-1	£9.99
Middlesex	1-85937-158-2	£14.99
New Forest	1-85937-128-0	£14.99
Newark (pb)	1-85937-366-6	£9.99
Newport, Wales (pb)	1-85937-258-9	£9.99
Newquay (pb)	1-85937-421-2	£9.99
Norfolk (pb)	1-85937-195-7	£9.99
Norfolk Living Memories	1-85937-217-1	£14.99
Northamptonshire	1-85937-150-7	£14.99
Northumberland Tyne & Wear (pb)	1-85937-281-3	£9.99
North Devon Coast	1-85937-146-9	£14.99
North Devon Living Memories	1-85937-261-9	£14.99
North London	1-85937-206-6	£14.99
North Wales (pb)	1-85937-298-8	£9.99
North Yorkshire (pb)	1-85937-236-8	£9.99
Norwich (pb)	1-85937-194-9	£8.99
Nottingham (pb)	1-85937-324-0	£9.99
Nottinghamshire (pb)	1-85937-187-6	£9.99
Oxford (pb)	1-85937-411-5	£9.99
Oxfordshire (pb)	1-85937-430-1	£9.99
Peak District (pb)	1-85937-280-5	£9.99
Penzance	1-85937-069-1	£12.99
Peterborough (pb)	1-85937-219-8	£9.99
Piers	1-85937-237-6	£17.99
Plymouth	1-85937-119-1	£12.99
Poole & Sandbanks (pb)	1-85937-251-1	£9.99
Preston (pb)	.1-85937-212-0	£9.99
Reading (pb)	1-85937-238-4	£9.99
Romford (pb)	1-85937-319-4	£9.99
Salisbury (pb)	1-85937-239-2	£9.99
Scarborough (pb)	1-85937-379-8	£9.99
St Albans (pb)	1-85937-341-0	£9.99
St Ives (pb)	1-85937415-8	£9.99
Scotland (pb)	1-85937-182-5	£9.99
Scottish Castles (pb)	1-85937-323-2	£9.99
Sevenoaks & Tunbridge	1-85937-057-8	£12.99
Sheffield, South Yorks (pb)	1-85937-267-8	£9.99
Shrewsbury (pb)	1-85937-325-9	£9.99
Shropshire (pb)	1-85937-326-7	£9.99
Somerset	1-85937-153-1	£14.99
South Devon Coast	1-85937-107-8	£14.99
South Devon Living Memories	1-85937-168-x	£14.99
South Hams	1-85937-220-1	£14.99
Southampton (pb)	1-85937-427-1	£9.99
Southport (pb)	1-85937-425-5	£9.99
Staffordshire	1-85937-047-0	£12.99
Stratford upon Avon	1-85937-098-5	£12.99
Suffolk (pb)	1-85937-221-x	£9.99
Suffolk Coast	1-85937-259-7	£14.99
Surrey (pb)	1-85937-240-6	£9.99
Sussex (pb)	1-85937-184-1	£9.99
Swansea (pb)	1-85937-167-1	£9.99
Tees Valley & Cleveland	1-85937-211-2	£14.99
Thanet (pb)	1-85937-116-7	£9.99
Tiverton (pb)	1-85937-178-7	£9.99
Torbay	1-85937-063-2	£12.99
Truro	1-85937-147-7	£12.99
Victorian and Edwardian Cornwall	1-85937-252-x	£14.99
Victorian & Edwardian Devon	1-85937-253-8	£14.99
Victorian & Edwardian Kent	1-85937-149-3	£14.99
Vic & Ed Maritime Album	1-85937-144-2	£17.99
Victorian and Edwardian Sussex	1-85937-157-4	£14.99
Victorian & Edwardian Yorkshire	1-85937-154-x	£14.99
Victorian Seaside	1-85937-159-0	£17.99
Villages of Devon (pb)	1-85937-293-7	£9.99
Villages of Kent (pb)	1-85937-294-5	£9.99
Villages of Sussex (pb)	1-85937-295-3	£9.99
Warwickshire (pb)	1-85937-203-1	£9.99
Welsh Castles (pb)	1-85937-322-4	£9.99
West Midlands (pb)	1-85937-289-9	£9.99
West Sussex	1-85937-148-5	£14.99
West Yorkshire (pb)	1-85937-201-5	£9.99
Weymouth (pb)	1-85937-209-0	£9.99
Wiltshire (pb)	1-85937-277-5	£9.99
Wiltshire Churches (pb)	1-85937-171-x	£9.99
Wiltshire Living Memories	1-85937-245-7	£14.99
Winchester (pb)	1-85937-428-x	£9.99
Windmills & Watermills	1-85937-242-2	£17.99
Worcester (pb)	1-85937-165-5	£9.99
Worcestershire	1-85937-152-3	£14.99
York (pb)	1-85937-199-x	£9.99
Yorkshire (pb)	1-85937-186-8	£9.99
Yorkshire Living Memories	1-85937-166-3	£14.99

See Frith books on the internet www.francisfrith.co.uk

FRITH PRODUCTS & SERVICES

Francis Frith would doubtless be pleased to know that the pioneering publishing venture he started in 1860 still continues today. A hundred and forty years later, The Francis Frith Collection continues in the same innovative tradition and is now one of the foremost publishers of vintage photographs in the world. Some of the current activities include:

Interior Decoration

Today Frith's photographs can be seen framed and as giant wall murals in thousands of pubs, restaurants, hotels, banks, retail stores and other public buildings throughout the country. In every case they enhance the unique local atmosphere of the places they depict and provide reminders of gentler days in an increasingly busy and frenetic world.

Product Promotions

Frith products are used by many major companies to promote the sales of their own products or to reinforce their own history and heritage. Frith promotions have been used by Hovis bread, Courage beers, Scots Porage Oats, Colman's mustard, Cadbury's foods, Mellow Birds coffee, Dunhill pipe tobacco, Guinness, and Bulmer's Cider.

Genealogy and Family History

As the interest in family history and roots grows world-wide, more and more people are turning to Frith's photographs of Great Britain for images of the towns, villages and streets where their ancestors lived; and, of course, photographs of the churches and chapels where their ancestors were christened, married and buried are an essential part of every genealogy tree and family album.

Frith Products

All Frith photographs are available Framed or just as Mounted Prints and Posters (size 23 x 16 inches). These may be ordered from the address below. From time to time other products - Address Books, Calendars, Table Mats, etc - are available.

The Internet

Already twenty thousand Frith photographs can be viewed and purchased on the internet through the Frith websites and a myriad of partner sites.

For more detailed information on Frith companies and products, look at these sites:

www.francisfrith.co.uk
www.francisfrith.com
(for North American visitors)

See the complete list of Frith Books at:
www.francisfrith.co.uk

This web site is regularly updated with the latest list of publications from the Frith Book Company. If you wish to buy books relating to another part of the country that your local bookshop does not stock, you may purchase on-line.

For further information, trade, or author enquiries please contact us at the address below:
The Francis Frith Collection, Frith's Barn, Teffont, Salisbury, Wiltshire, England SP3 5QP.
Tel: +44 (0)1722 716 376 Fax: +44 (0)1722 716 881 Email: sales@francisfrith.co.uk

See Frith books on the internet www.francisfrith.co.uk

TO RECEIVE YOUR FREE MOUNTED PRINT

Mounted Print
Overall size 14 x 11 inches

Cut out this Voucher and return it with your remittance for £1.95 to cover postage and handling, to UK addresses. For overseas addresses please include £4.00 post and handling. Choose any photograph included in this book. Your SEPIA print will be A4 in size, and mounted in a cream mount with burgundy rule line, overall size 14 x 11 inches.

Order additional Mounted Prints at HALF PRICE (only £7.49 each*)
If there are further pictures you would like to order, possibly as gifts for friends and family, purchase them at half price (no additional postage and handling required).

Have your Mounted Prints framed*
For an additional £14.95 per print you can have your chosen Mounted Print framed in an elegant polished wood and gilt moulding, overall size 16 x 13 inches (no additional postage and handling required).

*** IMPORTANT!**
These special prices are only available if ordered using the original voucher on this page (no copies permitted) and at the same time as your free Mounted Print, for delivery to the same address

Frith Collectors' Guild

From time to time we publish a magazine of news and stories about Frith photographs and further special offers of Frith products. If you would like 12 months FREE membership, please return this form.

Send completed forms to:
The Francis Frith Collection, Frith's Barn, Teffont, Salisbury, Wiltshire SP3 5QP

Voucher for FREE and Reduced Price Frith Prints

Picture no.	Page number	Qty	Mounted @ £7.49	Framed + £14.95	Total Cost
		1	Free of charge*	£	£
			£7.49	£	£
			£7.49	£	£
			£7.49	£	£
			£7.49	£	£
			£7.49	£	£
Please allow 28 days for delivery				*** Post & handling**	**£1.95**
Book Title				**Total Order Cost**	**£**

Please do not photocopy this voucher. Only the original is valid, so please cut it out and return it to us.

I enclose a cheque / postal order for £ ....
made payable to 'The Francis Frith Collection'
OR please debit my Mastercard / Visa / Switch / Amex card
(credit cards please on all overseas orders)

Number ....

Issue No (Switch only) .... Valid from (Amex/Switch) ....

Expires .... Signature ....

Name Mr/Mrs/Ms ....

Address ....

....

....

.... Postcode ....

Daytime Tel No .... Valid to 31/12/02

The Francis Frith Collectors' Guild

Please enrol me as a member for 12 months free of charge.

Name Mr/Mrs/Ms ....

Address ....

....

....

.... Postcode ....

Free Print - see overleaf

Would you like to find out more about Francis Frith?

We have recently recruited some entertaining speakers who are happy to visit local groups, clubs and societies to give an illustrated talk documenting Frith's travels and photographs. If you are a member of such a group and are interested in hosting a presentation, we would love to hear from you.

Our speakers bring with them a small selection of our local town and county books, together with sample prints. They are happy to take orders. A small proportion of the order value is donated to the group who have hosted the presentation. The talks are therefore an excellent way of fundraising for small groups and societies.

Can you help us with information about any of the Frith photographs in this book?

We are gradually compiling an historical record for each of the photographs in the Frith archive. It is always fascinating to find out the names of the people shown in the pictures, as well as insights into the shops, buildings and other features depicted.

If you recognize anyone in the photographs in this book, or if you have information not already included in the author's caption, do let us know. We would love to hear from you, and will try to publish it in future books or articles.

Our production team

Frith books are produced by a small dedicated team at offices in the converted Grade II listed 18th-century barn at Teffont near Salisbury, illustrated above. Most have worked with the Frith Collection for many years. All have in common one quality: they have a passion for the Frith Collection. The team is constantly expanding, but currently includes:

Jason Buck, John Buck, Douglas Burns, Heather Crisp, Isobel Hall, Rob Hames, Hazel Heaton, Peter Horne, James Kinnear, Tina Leary, Hannah Marsh, Eliza Sackett, Terence Sackett, Sandra Sanger, Shelley Tolcher, Susanna Walker, Clive Wathen and Jenny Wathen.